NO RAP: BOOK OF EMOTIONS PART 1 is a published work of Thomas Drake V. No part of this publication may be reproduced in whole or in part by any resources such as electronic, mechanical, photocopy, recording, or any other manner without written permission from Thomas Drake V.

Editor, Formatter, & Publisher:
J & I Publishing LLC

Address all inquiries to email:
tommygotpoems@gmail.com

Copyright © 2021 Thomas Drake V

All rights reserved.

ISBN: 978-1-7372056-0-9

NO RAP
BOOK OF EMOTIONS
PART 1

Thomas Drake V

TABLE OF CONTENTS

ACKNOWLEDGMENTS 1
Struggle, Black Man, Struggle 2-3
    Reflection 4-5
Hold On 6-7
    Reflection 8-9
Troubled Soul 10-11
    Reflection 12-13
Time Is Time 14-15
    Reflection 16-17
Sleeping with the Enemy 18-19
    Reflection 20-21
Pride 22-23
    Reflection 24-25

A Lonely Heart... 26-27
    Reflection.. 28-29
Aye, Nephew 30-31
    Reflection.. 32-33
My Darkest Moment 34-35
    Reflection.. 36-37
Wonderful Feeling 38-39
    Reflection.. 40-41
I Let Go 42-43
    Reflection.. 44-45
Blind Nigga 46-47
    Reflection.. 48-49
AUTHOR BIOGRAPHY 50-53

ACKNOWLEDGMENTS

First and foremost, let me thank God: without Him, none of this would be possible. I would like to thank my mom and dad, my sister, my grandma (RWG granny), and my kids. Next, I have to thank my "friends"—I wish them the best. In addition, I would like to thank my brother—I love you to death. Also, I cannot forget to thank the streets and the PA state correctional system. Last but not least, I would like to thank all my past relationships!

I say thank you with the deepest sincerity—without all of you, I wouldn't be who I am; not Thomas Drake V or Tommy Drake or even Drizzy! Thank you for the memories, experience and growth.

Struggle, Black Man, Struggle

Struggle, black man, struggle.

Odds aren't in your favor but all u know is get this paper.

Struggle, black man, struggle.

They say go to school to get ahead; my momma told me a closed mouth don't get fed,

I heard what she said …

Instead of asking, I learned

that if I got this and flipped that I could earn …

Struggle, black man, struggle.

What's good for you ain't good for me; the streets come with snakes and fleas.

A lot of niggaz was crips and bloods, but my niggaz was Gs.

Struggle, black man, struggle.

Life comes at you fast: some drown it with a flask; some cock it and blast.

I just want the money—check or cash—so it's make it or take it—ball or fake it.

Whatever it is, niggaz will hate it.

Struggle, black man, struggle.

Get knocked; do your time; gotta hold it down, can't fold now.

A 6x8, this is home now; the damn months turn to years, kids growing with tears.

This can't be life …

Struggle, black man, struggle.

Changed minds, changed lives, but this is the jungle and I'm trying to survive.

Niggaz rob and connive because they're scared to grind.

You wanna waste your life? Fine.

Struggle, black man, struggle.

What I lived, I can testify; other dudes choose to testify then turn around and justify

Like the shit's classified.

Naw, my nigga, you can't rectify …

Struggle, black man, struggle.

If you got outta the mud and you're done being a dud, I salute you,

'Cause these streets is slugs,

So I'm gonna play the cut and smoke my bud and mind my business while I run my business.

Struggle, Black Man, Struggle

Struggle, Black Man, Struggle

Reflection:

Struggle, black man, struggle—that's exactly what I did with every day of life! I struggled, and it was an uphill battle that I'm still fighting! Our life struggle is what molds us as men, what keeps us grounded. It says in the Bible, in Romans, God wants us to struggle to endure; endurance builds character, which gives us a hope (Romans 5:4, Contemporary English Version); meaning while we struggle, we're learning how to deal with struggle and to endure it. Our endurance is building us up for the next struggle.

I wrote about my struggle because I endured it—on the streets, in prison, in everyday life. I endured every bit of life's struggles; I figured out life with no teacher. We create our own struggles in life by choice: it's like the red pill or the blue pill, but no pill is the right pill because struggle will find you at any stage in life.

I just hope you understand your struggle because all struggles aren't the same. Like I said, this is the street: what's good for you isn't good for me! We have our own script already written; our decisions create our struggle. There's no such thing as life without struggle! Struggle is most black people's foundation; our history is full of struggle, black men hanged to death while other black men and women had to watch, or having to nurse their wife after she was raped repeatedly by some racist white man. Struggle, black man, struggle—that's all we know. Make the best of your struggle, like I'm trying to make the best of mine. Struggle, Black Man, Struggle.

Hold On

Like a river and a song, it all flows.
Just like a man needs his woman at his low.
God said every man reaps what he sows, but every man says he plays the game how it goes.
As men, we tell women we love them, but we refuse to grow.
But how so?
Even though we choose her to be ours, whether she is a queen or thot,
As men we just focus on giving her cock …
Excuse my language, but as men I think we forget the basics.
Even when we get smacked with the truth, we still can't face it.
That woman that loves you—hold on to my woman that loves me, hold on.
Dealing with a man can be like walking in the sand, showing traits you can't stand.
But you're still his number one fan, even while we act cornier than 2 Can Sam.
Straight fruit loops, the streets got our mind caged like Smokey in the chicken coop,
But if he loves you, he will adjust and fuck these niggaz ya girl who you should listen to.
Hold on to love and embrace it; hold on to your heart.

Wherever it goes, chase it.
Hold on to your sanity; hold to them tears you let go in front of that vanity.
Hold on for the better, 'cause men can change like the weather and it's cold—
You should get a sweater …
Confess your love—tell her, "We should be together."
Tell her all the things we could be together.
I don't know what my day would be like if we didn't see each other.
This world's getting sick; roles are changing,
Like men are asking questions and the women are explaining:
Like "Why are you just coming in? Like why couldn't you just be with me and stay in."
"Pause …"
Hold on to your morals and values fall back,
Turn down the volume, think before you speak, she still cooks what you eat;
You just don't know how many times she stared at you asleep and thought about smoking you. 'Cause you're thinking it's sweet, but you claim you're always on point out in these streets.
Hold on to her, take in her scent.
Hold on to her 'cause baby girl was heaven sent.
Hold on to her for better or for worse; hold on until you or her ride in that hearse.
Hold on, 'cause loving you is like a gift and a curse.
Hold on and always put your lady first.
Hold On

Hold On

Reflection:

I was just getting back into the swing of things, working on my second poem, my setup to get comfortable, to open myself up to what I was feeling, thinking and going through. I had envisioned a poem book with me telling all I was feeling and being creative. I also wanted to acknowledge my mental growth, my understanding of women and relationships, and to let women know us men make mistakes. We do dumb shit, we're not perfect, but if you love us, hold on.

Men aren't men until they accept fault in any situation, but men find it hard to do so. We lie, we sneak, we cheat, but a guaranteed fact is that we know where our heart is! It took me some time to value being with a good woman, like a woman who's really down for me. By the time I did, she didn't feel the same way about me as I did about her! You know the saying—women care too soon, men care too late; that's real as fuck! We men just be trying to fuck, and be lying while our dicks are stuck inside these women.

"I love you. I want you to have my baby. This is mine, this is your dick, you're the best" pumping straight gas, knowing we're going to say that to the next woman we put our dicks in.

We, as men, are losing our focus—the goal is to love, grow and build. Women expect us to be men, but, sadly, men are starting to act like women and the women are acting like men. It's truly sickening. Ladies, do me a favor—if you see potential, hold on. Men don't come around as fast as women. Hold on the streets had a hold on my thoughts and feelings; it had me cold in some way. I didn't understand what I was doing or saying. I was causing damage, but, ladies, I don't think you're blameless either. Hold on!

Troubled Soul

Troubled soul,

Mind so fucked up I need God to make me whole.

I got these thoughts in my head that are out of my control:

Like he used to be my friend

Now he's more like a foe

Like real bros, us before hoes ...

Troubled soul,

'Cause I've seen death.

There's no way to cope; my conscience is a mess.

On top of that I'm broke; how do I deal with the stress?

I can talk to my mom.

She would say, "Thank God that you are blessed..."

'Cause I've seen shit:

Like a man or woman saying to you they love you

And it don't mean shit,

'Cause at any moment they can be on some scheme shit,

Trying to get what you got,

Like they're on some fiend shit.

Troubled soul.

Damn, I really mean this.

I lost a lot of my niggaz; I would have never dreamed.
This soul trouble would be my reality.
You don't know the shit I deal with,
I got all types of anxiety coming up,
A young black man in this society
While the white man feeding me bullshit
Keep trying to lie to me.
Troubled soul,
'Cause my fiancée didn't feel like I treated her like she was Beyoncé.
I thought you was main like an entrée,
I love you with all my heart, that's all I'll say.
Troubled soul,
'Cause she don't see the vision.
I came a long way from being in that prison,
Far from that little boy who was prone to making bad decisions.
Listen ... My life was like a roller coaster,
But I always kept you close to my rib, like a shoulder holster.
Troubled soul,
I got demons.
I did some soul searching and I've been cleaning.
Lord God, build me up and tear me down like the seasons,
I won't resist my future is the reason.
Troubled Soul

Troubled Soul

Reflection:

Sitting on the edge of the bed at my ex's house before we split; before I actually knew our relationship was over, though I knew the direction it was headed. I was dealing with a mid-life crisis, I would say! I was growing; my heart was changing. I had just asked God for his will to be done in my life; I needed answers. I was depressed. I missed my grandmother and my childhood friend Devin Clark so bad, and I was having up and downs with the trucking company I had just started up. I was arguing every day with my ex. I would try to tell her my thoughts and mention some of the stuff that was bothering me internally, but all she would say was "You need a counselor." Meanwhile, I just wanted to confide in her, because I was finally ready to talk about my life.

My soul was troubled because I was changing and growing. I didn't feel about certain things like I used to anymore, plus I was starting to understand God, too. I started seeing what He was showing me; God was distancing my friends. He showed me I loved someone that could never love me, how I loved them! Me asking God for his help was me identifying that my soul was troubled and needed peace!

Time Is Time

Time is time.

Time doesn't stop.

I did my time by passing time and not watching the clock.

I sit back patient and observe like a hawk;

I plant seeds and I water my crop.

Time comes with a plan and a plot while I gather my thoughts,

Think long term and invest in my stock.

Time turned me into a better father,

I ain't looking for props.

The shit these kids do don't have me shocked

'Cause I remember how I was coming fresh outta the pot.

Time changes everything;

Time had me out here spending money on a wedding ring;

Time had me walk away from time I invested

'Cause over time my feelings started being neglected

And I couldn't accept it!
Time had me living a death wish until I created an exit;
You gotta respect it.
Time comes with growth.
Time can have you looking at the baddest bitch gross
Like I ain't feeling your ghost.
Time turned hoes to mother friends to brothers.
I've seen time bring things together;
I've also seen time have people change like the weather.
Time can't be repeated,
But time can have you looking back, feeling defeated.
Time is history.
Time can have us connecting dots like a mystery.
Time ain't no time if you've been to the penitentiary.
Time changed my heart.
Time had me ready to settle till death do us part.
Time had me change my ways;
I'm no longer a wolf or a shark, but I studied the art.
Time had me knowing my role and playing my part.
Time had me carrying a pole and slinging these darts.
Time's what you make it.
Time will have a nigga fake it till he makes it.
Time will have a nigga out here trying to take it.
Time comes with the good and the bad.
Fun times and sad times can make you appreciate everything you had!
Time Is Time

Time Is Time

Reflection:

Time is truly the physics of life; time is everything; I respect the fuck out of time, especially since I did time. Time is a reflection of time: past, future, present. Time comes with good and bad memories; it was me acknowledging time and all that came with it—my time in prison, me learning wisdom, me going through a breakup, and me starting a business.

This is my timeline to my life, my experience through time. Time speaks for itself—we go from young to old with time; time evolves us. Time is time, literally. When I was writing this, I swear it was like I was in a time capsule thinking about different time points in life that stuck out in my mind. When I did time, it was mind over matter. Yeah I was locked up but time was ticking, I got a date. Prison and time taught me patience; time gave me wisdom. My outlook on life is different because of time; my parenting changed over time due to time!

I remember the night before I wrote this poem. My grandma came to me in my dream—she had been gone about five years. This was the second time she came to me in a dream, both times with similar messages, but this time it triggered something inside of me. She said, "Boy, you the happiest kid I know, why you not happy? Why you not smiling?" I looked at my granny with tears and said, "I'm burnt out, Granny, I'm tired." She grabbed my hand and said (with her Southern accent), "Boyyyy, do you want me to kick your butt?" Then she broke out in her chuckle, I got a kick out of. Granny stopped with a serious face and said, "You got 'time'; you got plenty of time. Use it wisely. You got 'time'; you got time to change, fix, overcome, to be happy to be you! You got 'time'!"

Sleeping with the Enemy

Sleeping with the enemy,

I thought you was a friend to me.

Loved you like you was kin to me.

I was blinded by love; I should have seen the change in your energy.

Lonely thoughts make my heart ache; every thought of you makes my heart break.

Feelings of betrayal I just can't shake, but disrespect I can't take,

So I'm taking a stand; I got pride and I'm a man.

Sleeping with the enemy, knowing what you did to me.

Funny how you pretend to be when you know you're not into me.

We had a picture painted, I seen it so vividly.

I asked for God's help; I guess he ain't hearing me.

Knowing that you're cheating has put the biggest fear in me.

Damn …

Sleeping with the enemy, I sleep with my back to you

'Cause I'm still sexually attracted to you; It's hard to look at you without attacking on some freak shit.

I truly felt in my heart you was who I was going to be

with.

Time changes shit—pain, strain, shit:

I guess I'm gonna leave with the same thing I came with—nothing!

Mind confused with nothing to lose;

Everyone's slept around on me, I guess you hit the snooze …

But what hasn't killed me made me stronger; it taught me to go harder,

I got older and got smarter; I actually turned out better than my father.

My vision was short; now I see further.

Tell me why I bother when I'm sleeping with the enemy.

I really used to smoke niggaz like a chimney, pull up and ride like a jitney;

That's what I did to my enemy.

But this is a different war with different wounds and sores—

Why damage a heart that's pure?

I've been through so much; how much more do I have to endure?

I wish I was a bird so I could fly away and soar.

Instead, I'm human and I'm picking my heart up off the floor.

All the signs I ignored, thinking if I changed my behavior, you would change yours.

Sleeping with the Enemy

Sleeping with the Enemy

Reflection:

Watching a person go from being crazy about you to hating everything about you, from being your best friend, enjoying ups and downs with you, and building family ties with you, spending holidays and celebrating life, to lying in bed and you know you're sleeping with your enemy; looking at a person you completely don't know.

Your heart changes as you mature; things you once argued about seem meaningless. The killing of confidence, the constant disrespect, the constant accusing—these are actions of an enemy. An enemy can't share your happiness, feel sorrow or pain for you, because they wanna see you fail, they wanna see you hurt. This is what I laid beside for three out of seven years. I done my wrongs, I probably caused the hate, but I was never your enemy, I was never against you. I wonder how a person could fake it for so long—the audacity!

The hardest part about sleeping with the enemy is being attracted to someone that's emotionally empty toward you! I ignored the texts, the ignored phone calls, the sneaky links, the out-of-town trips, the jail visits. I ignored all those because I wasn't perfect nor innocent. I saw the bigger picture—maybe I accepted my karma—but the flip side is I felt disrespected, I felt betrayed, I felt less than a man for allowing it and lying in such discomfort. I slept with my back turned so I wouldn't have to look at you. I slept with my body facing the wall, same as I did when I was in jail, to force myself to sleep!

I was fighting a war I didn't know how to fight; this was a different type of beef. It was like emotional and spiritual warfare, like the more I changed, the more I matured, the more I evolved, the more humble I got and it helped me to realize I wasn't sleeping with someone I loved, I was sleeping with my enemy!

Pride

Pride is a stigma, pride is toxic,

Pride leaves us with a boxed-in logic.

Pride clouds vision and hinders our mind from making good and bad decisions.

Pride can cause division followed by subtraction,

Pride is two-thirds of your conscience like a fraction,

Pride can cause unwarranted action or reaction.

Pride is what stands between you and God,

Pride stops you from getting money 'cause you don't wanna work a certain job.

Pride's a façade; where was that pride when you was fighting these cases,

Standing and looking in all these white men's faces?

Pride turns us into a disgrace, doing anything to find our place.

Pride gives power to ignorance hidden by low self-esteem,
Pride blocks what's intended for you,
Pride blocks the vision of people depending on you.
I'm praying for you—please do me the honor of praying for me.
Pride was like a shackle while the real me waited to be freed;
I was blinded by pride, but now I can see.
Pride

Pride

Reflection:

Pride is most black people's kryptonite: we allow our pride to control situations, jobs, and life in general. We cannot stand in front of God with the pride we have! We have to be less full of pride; if we're less secure in ourselves, pride could be a form of insecurity. Pride puts shackles on you just like obesity or attention, etc! Pride is a form of ignorance, man.

This whole poem, I speak about myself and pride; I poetically address myself to pride and tell how my pride affected me. I had to let my pride go to make it to my next level; I knew that certain things couldn't make the journey and pride was one of them. I truly feel, to consider yourself a man, you must put your pride to the side.

I feel this is true for women as well, but some women are willing to put pride to the side. It's us men—our pride destroys shit. Me letting go of pride made me less evil, more understanding, more accountable, less boxed in. As an example, pride wouldn't let me walk away from an argument or someone disrespecting me. With no pride, I don't have a problem saying "I don't want any problems" or simply walking away. Me being less prideful is helping me find happiness and peace. Too much pride blocks blessings. The goal is less pride, more humility.

A Lonely Heart

A lonely heart—my heart was alive and beating till the hurt superseded.

I started feeling defeated, broken and depleted.

But I kept my head high: you would've had to look in my eyes to see my heart cry.

A lonely heart missing what it loves and can't have the empty feeling …

Heart broke from trials and tribulations—Lord, heal my wounds and lacerations.

A lonely heart—it beats and thrives,

Cautious from the hurt and crosses and the back-to-back losses.

A lonely heart I must protect at all costs.

I must defend my sanity, my heart crushed from the cards life handed me.

I feel branded, stuck, unable to move on with feelings I never spoke of.

I forgive, but I don't forget, and that's what hurts the memory—

the blatant disrespect and the images I start to reenact.

My face starts to turn up, heart beating fast; I ain't digging that.

A lonely heart wants and needs love, it wants to love back,

But everything seems like a trap—and that's a fact!

A lonely heart has to trust God, not flesh,

'Cause flesh is what got you into this mess—the questioning of self, and the stress.

A lonely heart that's conditioned itself to love and care through fear is a heart of faith and valor.

Even though it's lonely, you have a heart to be proud of.

A Lonely Heart

A Lonely Heart

Reflection:

I wrote this poem in three stages of emotion: lonely, hurt and empty. It took me a whole year to finish, even though it's probably one of my shorter poems, but the meaning of it means a lot to me. My life was in shambles, I was in a very dark place, but I felt it was important to document how I felt; to build strength, to learn, and to heal!

I had a rough life which I caused most of by just being an asshole, but my heart was always pure, I always loved others more than they loved me. Until I was 35, I wasn't able to accept that fact. I've had three committed relationships since I was 15, one of them with my kid's mother. All of my relationships ended with heartbreak and betrayal. My last relationship lasted seven years and it took the biggest toll on me and my heart! I lost myself in that relationship and found myself at the same time. I was so invested, committed to building a life together, I did shit I wouldn't have done if I didn't think it was forever.

But hey, you live, you learn, you heal. I couldn't have ever prepared myself for the feelings I was having; it was truly my first heartbreak as an adult and as a maturing man. It was rough trying to love a woman that looked you in your eyes and told you she wasn't happy and not in love no more, when you felt in your heart you were doing everything possible to keep it together plus dealing with unofficial friends and family! I literally put myself in a bubble—I had to cut ties and take a step back, but in that first step a lonely heart came. All I had was me to deal with my hurt, my imperfections, my lonely heart!

Aye, Nephew

Nephew, from day one you were my guy, my partner in crime,

You were that something in somebody we couldn't describe.

You were special, you touched everybody's heart who met you and weird to who didn't get you

Aye, nephew, I'm gonna miss you; this really hurts to my core beyond the tissue.

I wish we could talk to you again; I wish me, you and Tommy could go to our favorite spots again.

Aye, nephew, I always told you this was real life so be you and live life.

You didn't always get what I said so I said it twice—once tough and second nice.

Aye, nephew, I was your biggest fan; I watched you grow from playing ball to becoming a man.

I cheered you on, right beside your mom, and I screamed at you when you did something wrong Like not firing out or missing a block, and you would look and say, "I got you, unc."

Aye, nephew, getting you dressed for prom was fun; all you wanted was my jewels and cologne.

I got so many pictures on my phone.

I remember asking your date what time she was bringing you home.

And you said, "Chill, unc, I'm almost grown."

Aye, nephew, you were goofy and funny, tall and bubbly, you were different.

You didn't care who didn't like it and would say it in an instant.

Aye, nephew, I taught you how to get money; I taught you how to save and want more.

We cut grass together, we trucked together; I'm pretty sure we could have done more.

Aye, nephew, this life or the next life, I hope you're being true;

These was just a few of my good old memories of me and you.

Aye Nephew

Aye, Nephew

Reflection:

This was a call I wish I never got about something I wish my son had never seen. I was already dealing with heartbreak: life at this point was complete bullshit and nothing could go right for me. This phone call signed the deal; my heart broke all over again. "Dad, come back home; Chaka shot himself!" "What!? What do you mean he shot himself!" Son turns phone camera around. Nothing could've prepared me for seeing my nephew like that.

I'd driven to the west side of Pittsburgh; I hadn't been gone more than 45 minutes. I did 90mph back to my mom and dad's house. My sister was completely distraught. With my heart racing, I ran past her to go to my nephew, but the police blocked me and told me my nephew was gone. I cried liked I've never cried before. This was my nephew, my sister's first-born; he was like my own child, he looked up to me on so many levels. I was crushed.

Days later, sitting at the kitchen table with my mom trying to pick out pictures for his obituary, my mom asked me could I write a poem to be read at the funeral. I told her it would be my honor. I opened my phone and started talking to my nephew. Before I knew it, I'd written a full poem in 30 minutes.

"Aye, nephew" was how I greeted him, though I nicknamed him "Chak Nasty." That past summer we spent a lot of time together as we were both staying at my parents' house. I had the opportunity to school him on life, dress him for prom. He helped me start a landscaping business and we cut grass every day to make money. I was teaching him the hustle without being illegal; I was enjoying the chance to be hands-on with him. He was young, trying to find his way in life, playing, joking, not knowing what's serious and what isn't. I just wish there was more I could have done, more I could have said. My sister's heart will forever be broken!

RWG Chaka Raekwon Turner

My Darkest Moment

My darkest moment when I'm left to my thoughts,

That moment when I'm weak but I'm meek and strong as an ox

My darkest moment when I think back to my time in the box or the dudes I shot

My darkest moment was the lies I told; boy, was I bold!

Even when I was caught, I couldn't tell the truth about the drugs I sold or the hoes fold

I was playing a game 'cause this was the life I chose.

My darkest moment came with secrets and I would rather die before I leaked it.

I'm talking 'bout the type of shit that would leave you speechless.

In my darkest moment I had to stand tall like a man,

Like I would rather choose life in the can before I ever got on a stand.

But let me tell you about God's plan.

In my darkest, he gave me hope; when I was drowning, he sent a boat.

My darkest moment, I was challenged through the chaos;

I found balance, I found stability and peace through my malice.

A grown man that acted so childish.

My darkest moment came with growth and closure, but not before the exposure.

My darkest moment came with a journey and lessons followed by blessings,

which I'm open to receive.

My darkest moment is what made me strong, what made me whole, what changed my soul.

My Darkest Moment

My Darkest Moment

Reflection:

Sitting around, lost in my thoughts, trying to make sense of what was going on in my life – it lead me to my darkest moment! My darkest moment is a realization of how wrong I was living, at the same time taking accountability for my lifestyle and choices, the shit I've done. I could never speak of the people I've hurt, the time I lost to jail, the money I lost, the friends I lost – all are part of my darkest moment.

Once I changed my mindset, I started to see things differently; I started respecting life more. I've become more grounded about what's important and what isn't. I've become more spiritual, more in tune with myself. I can tell people now the reasons why I sold drugs and why I changed; why I was cheating in every relationship I was in, but played the victim when it was done to me. Being in my darkest moment felt bad, but it was good at the same time.

I feel like everything I went through molded me to be the man I'm trying to be today. My mother raised me to be strong and independent and to always think. When she would come visit me in jail, she would say, "Son, you need to see what God wants you to learn from this," and she would continue to say that throughout my trials and tribulations. Then one day it was clear, like a smack in the face; it was like I tapped into a different part of my brain overnight. I started seeing shit different, my feelings felt different; I loved different; I listened different; I comprehended different. It was like I went from dark to light!

Wonderful Feeling

I'm looking at you, I'm watching you sleep,

I'm feeling complete;

Your beauty skips my heartbeat—wonderful feeling.

The curves in your body got me thinking sexual healing.

Tell me how these hands and tongue kisses got you feeling.

Your smile and skin tone are most appealing—wow, what a wonderful feeling.

Looking into your eyes, staring into your brown pools, gives me the kid feeling from school—

Innocent and sweet humble and meek quiet, reserved and slightly a freak wonderful feeling.

Your company comforts me—I like how we go fast then slow down and you cum for me.

I've always been about my shit, can't let a nigga cum for me.

You're my Bonnie and I'm Clyde—let's do dash; come on a run with me.

Wonderful feeling looking at you, seeing a reflection and the sun beaming off your complexion.

See, baby, you're the queen and I'm your protection.

We gotta plan, baby, we can't take no misdirection or interception,

So let's fix and make correction.

Wonderful feeling listening to you talk;

Hearing what you're saying got me thinking damn …

I'm a lucky-ass man,

'Cause we're really on some build shit.

A few years back, I was on some kill shit—the streets had me so cold I couldn't feel shit.

That's real shit …

Wonderful feeling, seeing your ambition, seeing you put a gap between you and other bitches

Like there's no competition and when your mind is made up, you're relentless—I dig it.

Wonderful feeling love is, love. Love is happy, not sad.

Love is what you gave and it was more love than I ever had.

Wonderful Feeling

Wonderful Feeling

Reflection:

Sitting on a balcony in my two-bedroom villa in Orlando, Florida, on blunt number two. I stood up and looked through the glass sliding doors, watching the person I loved with all my heart sleeping peacefully. I stood there hitting my blunt hard with tears in my eyes, wondering what I could do to save my relationship!

I remember the feeling I had looking at her sleeping—it was warm and tingly; it was a wonderful feeling. It had been years since I wrote poetry and I had just written two to help me get my feelings out because I truly had nobody to let it out to, so I stood outside looking through the sliding glass doors and wrote what I felt. I wasn't good at expressing my feelings anymore; I had shut down a little from shit that was said or done to me. I just wanted to keep the peace, repair what was broke and get back to that wonderful feeling.

Me cutting ties with the street came with a big changing of the heart, changing of attitude, changing of reality. In the windstorm of things, I felt I owed her for my change and growth. Meanwhile, everything that was happening I prayed for. I guessed this was what hurt felt like, but I wanted to find the good.

Maybe it was the memories that gave me that wonderful feeling. It was a long road and I'd seen it coming to an end right then in that present moment. We're in a family setting with our children, enjoying vacation in a time share we purchased together. The wonderful feeling could have been what it could be; maybe the vision I'd seen for us was the wonderful feeling. Who knows? Maybe it was the thought in that moment, the setting, the vibe!

I Let Go

Today is the day I let go of the hurt, the lies and memories.

When I'm gone, y'all remember me—I let go of everything that was killing me.

My heart is no longer your hostage chained by emotions;

I no longer drink from your cup of evil potion.

You had me trapped like a rodent, but I'm no animal.

Love has run its course and that's understandable.

I've seen a future that's more than obtainable,

But you found traits in me that were hateable, I let go…

I let go of the good and bad, 'cause you forgot the bond we had.

I came a long way on my journey from court cases and paying attorneys

To creating a life that could last for eternities.

I let go: no more hoping and wishing; no more hugging and kissing.

We became too distant.

I remember trying to tell you my thoughts, but in my heart I felt like you didn't listen.

You don't have an idea what it's like to try to beat the system,

'Cause you will pack up and leave when the situation isn't fitting.

Our life and our purpose have already been written

And any time we're slipping, we can ask forgiveness.

I let go … I let go for my sanity even though the love in my heart for you has branded me.

I let go … I let go and choose peace—no more ill feelings or beef—

Because with or without you, I'm going to become who I'm destined to be!

We have come to a crossroads where our roads no longer meet.

Deceit and betrayal is where we failed; we had a lack of communication

So with these words, I submit my resignation: I let go…

Letting go for me is harder than you think, 'cause I've been in rough water and never did I sink.

I lost myself in you and you didn't even blink.

I let go … I let go, but I still love your daughter as my own

Even though mine can't even hear your voice on the phone,

And that type of selfishness I can't condone.

They wonder why you don't love 'em and I have no clue what I should tell 'em

So I let it go.

My goal was always to create something stationary, not temporary,

But somehow I created something contemporary.

Every move I thought I made was for the betterment of us!

Us means nothing if it's not valued and you'd rather live life as a vacuum

I Let Go…!

I Let Go

Reflection:

I was an emotional wreck, trying to come to terms with the reality that it was over. No more us, no more you and me. It was so hard to accept; I couldn't believe our seven-year run was just over, with nothing left in the tank. Watching her move on with ease, dating this guy, that guy. Questioning myself was getting too much to handle. I was talking to several women, but it was just to fill a void, just to put a Band-Aid on the wound.

I missed what I loved so much, but I trusted God. He kept telling me to let go, let go for so many reasons, for your sanity. Let go of the disrespect, let go of the hurt. Speak your heart, write your heart, let go. In the dark, lying across the bed in my mom and dad's guest room, I wrote, I let go … and expressed poetically everything I was feeling. I let go of the history. We had really built a ladder and started climbing up that shit together. To watch it tumble, I had to let go.

God opened my eyes so much along my journey; letting go was my destiny, letting go was God's will. God knew the person I was and the man I was becoming and if I didn't let go, I would never have peace. I would never be in control of my direction. I had to let go!

Blind Nigga

Blind nigga …

Is this political speaking or a physical state of mind?

I'm from the hood, I know both kinds—a lot of woke, but still blind niggaz …

No matter the crime, no matter the time; if you do it all again, you're still a blind nigga …

Being woke is a conscious state.

Putting something over your eyes makes you blind.

Let's see the decision your conscious makes.

I don't have to mention the struggle our mind can take,

'Cause I was chained and imprisoned to see if my soul would break.

I was woke, but I was blind.

When I was broke, my first thought was to go grind,

Listening to Scarface telling me the world was mine.

Boy, was I blind … a blind nigga …

Blind leads the blind, woke leads the woke—let that soak!

We're only woke to our blinds …

Us noticing our blinds, is this what makes us woke?

No, because as long as you're black in America, you'll always be a blind nigga …

We were brought here in chains on ships; we went from riches to shit.

How much blinder could we get?

We think the world is round 'cause of a white man.

We believe in Jesus 'cause of a white man.

So what does that make us? A blind … nigga.

Being woke is cool with some folk, but you got the blind tell n woke jokes

And we wonder why our youth's so cutthroat on social media

Posting pistols like a gun show to prison where they're trying to go.

Blind nigga …

Love is love, don't let love make you blind, nigga.

They say if you search, you will find yourself, I hope you find nigga.

Rather, if you're woke or blind, nigga, knowledge is power, blind nigga …

You can turn on the TV and see crackers frying niggaz

You see how my black people are dying, nigga.

We're all BLIND, NIGGA!

Blind Nigga

Reflection:

I caught myself tapping into my versatility but ended up taking the intro line seriously. "Is this politics speaking or a physical state of mind?" I took it as me asking myself the question and replied, we're all blind niggaz, we're all blind to what's going on in front of us. A white person will say why don't you go back where you came from when y'all brought us here on a boat and gave us religion. Meanwhile, they claimed land they didn't discover. Blind? They think we're dumb niggaz.

We're so blind we pray to a blond-haired, blue-eyed man as God when it clearly says his feet was like copper and his hair like wool. Sounds like a person of color to me. We live every day blind, but why not wake up and see that being blind is a choice. Blind is lack of knowledge, blind is us thinking Black Lives Matter when it's a fact in America that black lives don't matter. Do I have to say their names?!

Us young parents are losing our kids at a fast rate because we're blind. These kids didn't get a chance to see because they were born blind; they only see what's in front of them, blind to the hidden agenda. I told you we were blind, niggaz!

AUTHOR BIOGRAPHY

I grew up on the east side of Pittsburgh, PA, in the metropolitan area called Wilkinsburg. Son of Thomas IV and Darlene Drake, I was ambitious from a young age. I always wanted more and wanted to see past the world of Wilkinsburg. I graduated from Wilkinsburg High in 2002 and became a father to my first-born son, Thomas Drake VI, in 2004. I become a father twice while incarcerated. After serving a year, I came home from the Allegheny County Jail in May of 2005, but by 2006 I was back in jail and I became a father again to my first-born daughter, Kamyah Drake, in May of 2007. The following winter I was sent to Pennsylvania State Correction at Gater Ford, where I figured out what I wanted to do with my life. In June of 2009 I was released and reunited with my son and the two-year-old daughter I had never met. The following September I enrolled in the Empire School of Beauty, which I completed a year later, now a father of three with my second daughter, Sariyah Drake.

By that time I was full blown into my double life wins and losses, and in spring of 2012 I was arrested on five warrants dating back to 2010 and 11 for controlled drug buys to a confidential informant. Later that year I found myself in more trouble— trouble that changed my life and views forever.

I had a heart-to-heart talk with myself and knew I needed more out of life than jail and court fees. I applied to All State and Career and obtained my class A CDL truck driver's license within 30 days. From there my journey of change was invented. In March of 2013 I got my first trucking job for Folino

Construction (TDF Transport), where my vision was born—I knew where my life was headed, what I wanted to do, and how I wanted to it. I worked different trucking jobs until I bought my own winter of 2015—the best decision of my life!!!

I first got into poetry in the 12th grade, when I wrote a poem called "what's love" and my history teacher read it, copied it, and framed it in her classroom. When I first started having my kids, I used to write poetry all the time. During my bid in jail, I once got locked in my room on a 48-hour lockdown as a poet, and came out a rapper! I wanted to rap so badly when I came home, I tried to pursue a rap career, but never released any of the material due to lack of support. In 2016 I gave up that dream completely to focus on my career and business. But in winter of 2018 I started writing poetry again. I wanted to write my emotions. I wanted to write my feelings. I wanted to share my growth and wisdom. I finally wanted to be what my mom said I would be, years before: a writer!

NO RAP: BOOK OF EMOTIONS PART 1 **is my first book. If I had to choose my favorite poem from this book it would be Pride"—for years I lived with too much of it. For what reason? I have no clue, but I knew that on the path I was on, I couldn't take it with me, that's for sure! My advice? Be careful what you pray for and be ready for what you're praying for! God's going to give you everything you ask for! "Struggle, Black Man, Struggle" was my first poem for this book and "Hold On" was my second. Both were significant to me, as at the time I was struggling with a lifestyle I no longer wanted to live or be a part of, and wanting the woman I loved at the time to hold on! I'm going to continue to write and express myself through poetry; this is just the beginning.**

~Thomas Drake V

www.ingramcontent.com/pod-product-compliance
Lightning Source LLC
Chambersburg PA
CBHW051948160426
43198CB00013B/2361